LA RAKONTO DE L' NOMBROJ

THE NUMBER STORY

SMALL BOOK ONE

ENGLISH - ESPERANTO

Numbers Teach Children Their Number Names

written and illustrated by

MISS ANNA

Early Reader Edition of *The Number Story 1*
Bronze Medal Winner, 2016 Wishing Shelf Book Award

Cover by | Lumpy Publishing
Layout by | Lumpy Publishing
Translated by Ksandero Ksan Paŭl
Coloring by Jieeun Woo and Maria Mirabella

Library of Congress Control Number: 2018902040

Names: Miss Anna, author.
Title: Number story : numbers teach children their number names / Miss Anna.
Description: Portland, OR: Lumpy Publishing, 2018.
Identifiers: ISBN 978-0-9962164-6-3| LCCN 2018902040
Summary: The pictures and rhymes present stories which introduce numbers 0-10.
Subjects: LCSH Numeration—English--Esperanto--Pictorial works--Juvenile literature. | BISAC JUVENILE NONFICTION /
Languages: English--Esperanto
Classification: LCC QA141.3 .M57 2018 | DDC 513—dc23

Publisher: Lumpy Publishing
Website: www.missannabooks.com
Email: missanna@missannabooks.com

Paperback: ISBN 978-0-9962164-6-3
Printed in the U.S.A.   1 3 5 7 9 10 8 6 4 2

Ĉu vi volas lerni
la nomojn de Nombroj?

It is very easy and a lot of fun!

Estas facile kaj tre amuze!

Say-along our little jingle

Kantu kun ni niajn rakonteton!

starting from Number One!

Ni komencu de Nombro Unu!

1

ONE looks like my one finger.

UNU

aspektas kiel fingro mia.

ONE!
UNU!

2

TWO trails a tail.

DU

havas voston kiel spanielo.

A TAIL! VOSTO!

3

THREE   has bumps.

TRI

estas monteto kun ĝemelo kopia.

Rigardu la verdajn montetojn!

4

FOUR   carries a sail.

KVAR

estas boato—jen ties velo.

A SAIL!
VELO!

5

FIVE is a racing track.

KVIN

estas dromo por aŭtomobilo.

VROOM
VRRRRM!

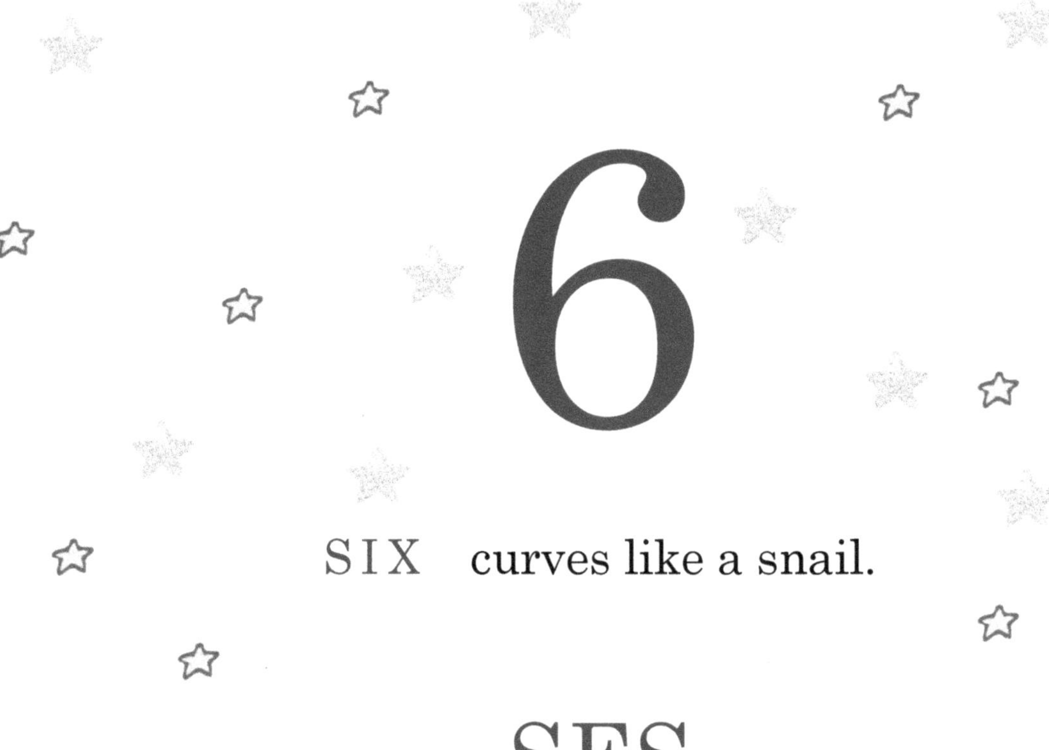

6

S I X curves like a snail.

SES

fleksiĝas kiel limako ŝlimiga.

A SNAIL! LIMAKO!

7

SEVEN has a sharp angle.

SEP

estas akra, kiel hakilo.

BE CAREFUL! IT'S SHARP!
Singardu! Ĝi akras!

8

EIGHT   is rollercoaster rails.

OK

estas onda fervojo timiga.

HURA!
YIPPEE!

NINE   is a bubble on a stick.

NAŬ

estas bobelo sur stangeto.

A BUBBLE!

BOBELO!

10

TEN   is an eye of a whale.

DEK

estas unu okulo baleno.

WINK!
OKULSIGNON!
HELLO! SALUTON!

And
Kaj

0

ZERO   is an empty pail.

NUL

estas sitelo malplena.

IT'S
EMPTY!
ĜI
MALPLENAS!

Thank you for playing with us today.

We had a lot of fun too!

Dankon, ke vi ludis kun ni hodiaŭ

Ni multe amuziĝis ankaŭ!

We are your Number friends,
Zero to Ten,
Who will be here for you~
Ni estas viaj Nombraj geamikoj
Nul al Dek.
Ni ĉiam ĉeestos por vi.

Bye-bye now!
See you again soon!
Adiaŭ!
Ĝis baldaŭ!

The Numbers are *SINGING* too!

To sing-a-long, look for Miss Anna Number Story
at your favorite music store like iTUNES.

MP3

Numbers 0-10
IDENTIFYING
& COUNTING

Numbers 11-20
& Ordinals
first, second, third...

Numbers 0-100
& Place Values
ones, tens, hundreds...

About Clock
& Telling Tim
hours, minutes, seco

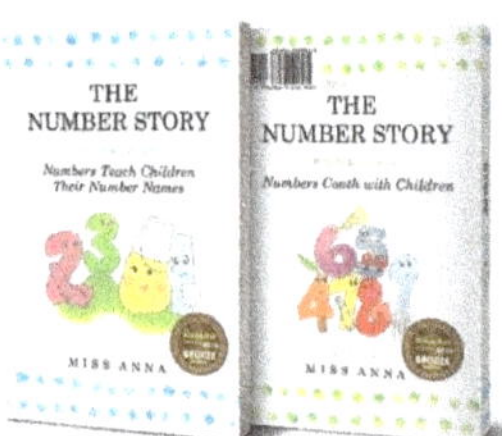

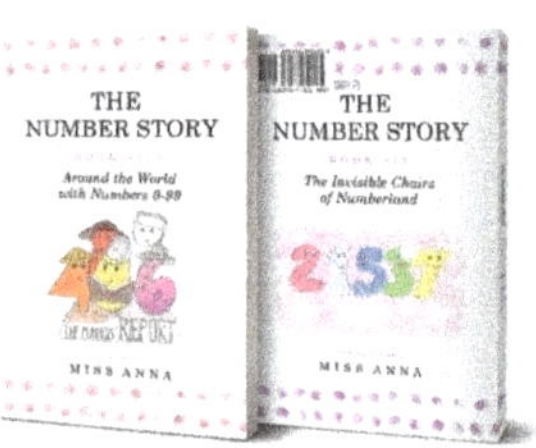

Number Story 1 & 2
isbn: 978-0-996216-48-7

Number Story 3 & 4
isbn: 978-1-945977-01-5

Number Story 5 & 6
isbn: 978-1-945977-06-0

Number Story 7 &
isbn: 978-1-949320-4

For more Miss Anna books to love,
visit us at

www.missannabooks.com

Numbers are working hard all over the world!
Come Travel the World with Us!

www.ingramcontent.com/pod-product-compliance
Lightning Source LLC
Chambersburg PA
CBHW041101050726

47599CB00018B/2221